2008 SUPPLEMENT

CONSTITUTIONAL LAW

SIXTEENTH EDITION

by

KATHLEEN M. SULLIVAN
Former Dean of the School of Law,
Stanley Morrison Professor of Law, and
Director, Constitutional Law Center,
Stanford University

GERALD GUNTHER
Late William Nelson Cromwell Professor of Law Emeritus
Stanford University

FOUNDATION PRESS
75TH ANNIVERSARY

THOMSON

WEST

© 2008 By THOMSON REUTERS/FOUNDATION PRESS
                              395 Hudson Street
                              New York, NY 10014
                              Phone Toll Free 1–877–888–1330
                              Fax (212) 367–6799
                              foundation–press.com
Printed in the United States of America

ISBN 978–1–59941–522–2

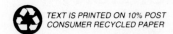 TEXT IS PRINTED ON 10% POST CONSUMER RECYCLED PAPER

TABLE OF CONTENTS

Page numbers on the left indicate where the new cases fit into the casebook. Principal cases are in **bold face**.

*

TABLE OF CASES

Principal cases are in bold type. Non-principal cases are in roman type. References are to Pages.

*

2008 SUPPLEMENT

CONSTITUTIONAL LAW

*

CHAPTER 5

FEDERAL LIMITS ON STATE REGULATION OF INTERSTATE COMMERCE

SECTION 1. THE DORMANT COMMERCE CLAUSE

Page 202. Add after Note 3:

4. *Differential taxation of municipal bonds.* To what other public functions might United Haulers apply besides waste hauling? In DEPARTMENT OF REVENUE OF KENTUCKY v. DAVIS, ___ U.S. ___, 128 S.Ct. 1801 (2008), the Court considered a Dormant Commerce Clause challenge to a differential scheme by which Kentucky exempted interest on its own public bonds from state income taxes but imposed such taxes on bond interest from other States. Billions of dollars of capital was at stake in the case, as 36 States took the same approach as Kentucky, five others took similar approaches, and all 49 other States filed an amicus curiae brief in its support.

A majority of the Court rejected the challenge and upheld the law, with Justice SOUTER delivering the judgment of the Court. In a portion of his opinion joined by Chief Justice Roberts and Justices Stevens, Scalia, Breyer and Ginsburg, he found the case governed by United Haulers: "In United Haulers, we explained that a government function is not susceptible to standard dormant Commerce Clause scrutiny owing to its likely motivation by legitimate objectives distinct from the simple economic protectionism the Clause abhors. This logic applies with even greater force to laws favoring a State's municipal bonds, given that the issuance of debt securities to pay for public projects is a quintessentially public function, with [a] venerable history. [By] issuing bonds, state and local governments 'sprea[d] the costs of public projects over time,' much as one might buy a house with a loan subject to monthly payments. Bonds place the cost of a project on the citizens who benefit from it over the years, and they allow for public work beyond what current revenues could support. Bond proceeds are thus the way to shoulder the cardinal civic responsibilities listed in United Haulers: protecting the health, safety, and welfare of citizens. [Thus,] United Haulers provides a firm basis for reversal. Just like the ordinances upheld there, Kentucky's tax exemption favors a traditional government function without any differential treatment favoring local entities over substantially similar out-of-state interests."

Justice KENNEDY, joined by Justice Alito, filed a dissent, objecting to United Haulers as an "unfortunate recent exception" to the presumption against laws facially discriminating against out-of-state commerce: "The Court defends the Kentucky law by explaining that it serves a traditional government function and concerns the 'cardinal civic responsibilities' of protecting health, safety, and welfare. This is but a reformulation of the phrase 'police power,' long abandoned as a mere tautology. It is difficult to identify any state law that has come before us that would not meet the Court's description. [The] tax imposed here is an explicit discrimination against out-of-state issuances for admitted protectionist purposes. It cannot be sustained unless the Court disavows the discrimination principle, one of the most important protections we have elaborated for the Nation's interstate markets." Justice Kennedy objected that the majority "overlooks the argument that was central to the entire holding of United Haulers. There the Court concluded the ordinance applied equally to interstate and in-state commerce [because] the government had monopolized the waste processing industry. Nondiscrimination, not just state involvement, was central to the rationale. That justification cannot be invoked here, for discrimination against out-of-state bonds is the whole purpose of the law in question. Kentucky has not monopolized the bond market or the municipal bond market. Kentucky has entered a competitive, nonmonopolized market and, to give its bonds a market advantage, has taxed out-of-state municipal bonds at a higher rate. [This] case is not an extension of United Haulers; it is a rejection of its principal rationale—that in monopolizing the local market, the ordinance applied equally to interstate and local commerce."

In a portion of his opinion representing a plurality consisting only of himself and Justices Stevens and Breyer, Justice Souter defended the Kentucky law on the alternative ground that, in issuing the tax-exempt bonds in the first place, the State was acting as a market participant rather than a market regulator, and thus was entitled to prefer its own state residents. The dissent objected that bond interest taxation, not bond issuance, was the relevant event. Justice Thomas filed a concurrence in the judgment expressing the view that the Court generally lacks authority to invalidate state laws under the Dormant Commerce Clause.

CHAPTER 6

SEPARATION OF POWERS

SECTION 2. EXECUTIVE DISCRETION IN TIMES OF WAR OR
TERRORISM

Page 291.   Add to end of Note 3:

In a decision issued toward the end of the October 2007 Term, a narrowly divided Court reversed that decision, reaching the question whether the Military Commissions Act (MCA), as modified by the Detainee Treatment Act (DTA), unconstitutionally suspends the writ of habeas corpus. Section 7 of the MCA provides: "No court, justice, or judge shall have jurisdiction to hear or consider an application for a writ of habeas corpus filed by or on behalf of an alien detained by the United States who has been determined by the United States to have been properly detained as an enemy combatant or is awaiting such determination." The DTA provides for the exclusive jurisdiction of the Court of Appeals for the District of Columbia Circuit to review decisions by CSRTs concerning alien enemy combatants.

Boumediene v. Bush

___ U.S. ___, 128 S.Ct. 2229 (2008).

Justice KENNEDY delivered the opinion of the Court, in which Justices STEVENS, SOUTER, GINSBURG, and BREYER joined.

Petitioners are aliens designated as enemy combatants and detained at the United States Naval Station at Guantanamo Bay, Cuba. [Petitioners] present a question not resolved by our earlier cases relating to the detention of aliens at Guantanamo: whether they have the constitutional privilege of habeas corpus, a privilege not to be withdrawn except in conformance with the Suspension Clause, Art. I, § 9, cl. 2. We hold these petitioners do have the habeas corpus privilege. Congress has enacted a statute, the Detainee Treatment Act of 2005 (DTA), that provides certain procedures for review of the detainees' status. We hold that those procedures are not an adequate and effective substitute for habeas corpus. Therefore § 7 of the Military Commissions Act of 2006 (MCA) operates as an unconstitutional suspension of the writ.

II.   [As] a threshold matter, we must decide whether MCA § 7 denies the federal courts jurisdiction to hear habeas corpus actions pending at the time of its enactment. We hold the statute does deny that jurisdiction, so that, if the statute is valid, petitioners' cases must be dismissed.

III.   [In] deciding the constitutional questions now presented we must determine whether petitioners are barred from seeking the writ or invoking the protections of the Suspension Clause either because of their status, *i.e.*, petitioners' designation by the Executive Branch as enemy combatants, or their physical location, *i.e.*, their presence at Guantanamo Bay.

A.   [The] Framers viewed freedom from unlawful restraint as a fundamental precept of liberty, and they understood the writ of habeas corpus as a vital instrument to secure that freedom. Experience taught, however, that the common-law writ all too often had been insufficient to guard against the abuse of monarchial power. That history counseled the necessity for specific language in the Constitution to secure the writ and ensure its place in our legal system. [That] the Framers considered the writ a vital instrument for the protection of individual liberty is evident from the care taken to specify the limited grounds for its suspension: "The Privilege of the Writ of Habeas Corpus shall not be suspended, unless when in Cases of Rebellion or Invasion the public Safety may require it." Art. I, § 9, cl. 2.

[The] Clause protects the rights of the detained by a means consistent with the essential design of the Constitution. It ensures that, except during periods of formal suspension, the Judiciary will have a time-tested device, the writ, to maintain the "delicate balance of governance" that is itself the surest safeguard of liberty. The Clause protects the rights of the detained by affirming the duty and authority of the Judiciary to call the jailer to account. The separation-of-powers doctrine, and the history that influenced its design, therefore must inform the reach and purpose of the Suspension Clause.

B.   ["At] the absolute minimum" the Clause protects the writ as it existed when the Constitution was drafted and ratified. [The] Government argues the common-law writ ran only to those territories over which the Crown was sovereign. Petitioners argue that jurisdiction followed the King's officers. Diligent search by all parties reveals no certain conclusions. In none of the cases cited do we find that a common-law court would or would not have granted, or refused to hear for lack of jurisdiction, a petition for a writ of habeas corpus brought by a prisoner deemed an enemy combatant, under a standard like the one the Department of Defense has used in these cases, and when held in a territory, like Guantanamo, over which the Government has total military and civil control. [Each] side in the present matter argues that the very lack of a precedent on point supports its position. The Government points out there is no evidence that a court sitting in England granted habeas relief to an enemy alien detained abroad; petitioners respond there is no evidence that a court refused to do so for lack of jurisdiction. [We decline] to infer too much, one way or the other, from the lack of historical evidence on point.

IV.   [Drawing] from its position that at common law the writ ran only to territories over which the Crown was sovereign, the Government says the Suspension Clause affords petitioners no rights because the United States does not claim sovereignty over the place of detention. Guantanamo Bay is not formally part of the United States. [We] accept the Government's position that Cuba, and not the United States, retains de jure sovereignty over Guantanamo Bay. As we did in Rasul, however, we take notice of the obvious and uncontested fact that the United States, by virtue of its complete jurisdiction and control over the base, maintains de facto sovereignty over this territory.

A. [The] Court has discussed the issue of the Constitution's extraterritorial application on many occasions. These decisions undermine the Government's argument that, at least as applied to noncitizens, the Constitution necessarily stops where de jure sovereignty ends. [Nothing] in Eisentrager says that de jure sovereignty is or has ever been the only relevant consideration in determining the geographic reach of the Constitution or of habeas corpus. [Questions] of extraterritoriality turn on objective factors and practical concerns, not formalism.

B. The Government's formal sovereignty-based test raises troubling separation-of-powers concerns as well. The political history of Guantanamo illustrates the deficiencies of this approach. The United States has maintained complete and uninterrupted control of the bay for over 100 years. At the close of the Spanish–American War, Spain ceded control over the entire island of Cuba to the United States and specifically "relinquishe[d] all claim[s] of sovereignty ... and title." [Although] it recognized, by entering into the 1903 Lease Agreement, that Cuba retained "ultimate sovereignty" over Guantanamo, the United States continued to maintain the same plenary control it had enjoyed since 1898. [The] Constitution grants Congress and the President the power to acquire, dispose of, and govern territory, not the power to decide when and where its terms apply. Even when the United States acts outside its borders, its powers are not "absolute and unlimited" but are subject "to such restrictions as are expressed in the Constitution."

C. [At] least three factors are relevant in determining the reach of the Suspension Clause: (1) the citizenship and status of the detainee and the adequacy of the process through which that status determination was made; (2) the nature of the sites where apprehension and then detention took place; and (3) the practical obstacles inherent in resolving the prisoner's entitlement to the writ.

Applying this framework, we note at the onset that the status of these detainees is a matter of dispute. The petitioners, like those in Eisentrager, are not American citizens. But the petitioners in Eisentrager did not contest, it seems, the Court's assertion that they were "enemy alien[s]." In the instant cases, by contrast, the detainees deny they are enemy combatants. [As] to the second factor relevant to this analysis, the detainees here are similarly situated to the Eisentrager petitioners in that the sites of their apprehension and detention are technically outside the sovereign territory of the United States, [a] factor that weighs against finding they have rights under the Suspension Clause. But there are critical differences between Landsberg Prison, circa 1950, and the United States Naval Station at Guantanamo Bay in 2008. Unlike its present control over the naval station, the United States' control over the prison in Germany was neither absolute nor indefinite. [In] every practical sense Guantanamo is not abroad; it is within the constant jurisdiction of the United States. [As] to the third factor, we recognize, as the Court did in Eisentrager, that there are costs to holding the Suspension Clause applicable in a case of military detention abroad. Habeas corpus proceedings may require expenditure of funds by the Government and may divert the attention of military personnel from other pressing tasks. While we are sensitive to these concerns, we do not find them dispositive. Compliance with any judicial process requires some incremental expenditure of resources.

[We] hold that Art. I, § 9, cl. 2, of the Constitution has full effect at Guantanamo Bay. If the privilege of habeas corpus is to be denied to the detainees now before us, Congress must act in accordance with the requirements of the Suspension Clause. [The] MCA does not purport to be a formal suspension of the writ; and the Government, in its submissions to us, has not argued that it is. Petitioners, therefore, are entitled to the privilege of habeas corpus to challenge the legality of their detention.

V.   In light of this holding the question becomes whether the statute stripping jurisdiction to issue the writ avoids the Suspension Clause mandate because Congress has provided adequate substitute procedures for habeas corpus. [When] Congress has intended to replace traditional habeas corpus with habeas-like substitutes, [it] has granted to the courts broad remedial powers to secure the historic office of the writ. [In] contrast the DTA's jurisdictional grant is quite limited. The Court of Appeals has jurisdiction not to inquire into the legality of the detention generally but only to assess whether the CSRT complied with the "standards and procedures specified by the Secretary of Defense" and whether those standards and procedures are lawful. If Congress had envisioned DTA review as coextensive with traditional habeas corpus, it would not have drafted the statute in this manner.

B.   We do not endeavor to offer a comprehensive summary of the requisites for an adequate substitute for habeas corpus. We do consider it uncontroversial, however, that the privilege of habeas corpus entitles the prisoner to a meaningful opportunity to demonstrate that he is being held pursuant to "the erroneous application or interpretation" of relevant law. [We hold] that when the judicial power to issue habeas corpus properly is invoked the judicial officer must have adequate authority to make a determination in light of the relevant law and facts and to formulate and issue appropriate orders for relief, including, if necessary, an order directing the prisoner's release.

C.   [Even assuming] the DTA can be construed to allow the Court of Appeals to review or correct the CSRT's factual determinations, as opposed to merely certifying that the tribunal applied the correct standard of proof, we see no way to construe the statute to allow what is also constitutionally required in this context: an opportunity for the detainee to present relevant exculpatory evidence that was not made part of the record in the earlier proceedings. [This] evidence, however, may be critical to the detainee's argument that he is not an enemy combatant and there is no cause to detain him. [Petitioners] have met their burden of establishing that the DTA review process is, on its face, an inadequate substitute for habeas corpus.

IV.A. [The] question remains whether there are prudential barriers to habeas corpus review under these circumstances. [In] some of these cases six years have elapsed without the judicial oversight that habeas corpus or an adequate substitute demands. And there has been no showing that the Executive faces such onerous burdens that it cannot respond to habeas corpus actions. [While] some delay in fashioning new procedures is unavoidable, the costs of delay can no longer be borne by those who are held in custody. The detainees in these cases are entitled to a prompt habeas corpus hearing.

[Our] opinion does not undermine the Executive's powers as Commander in Chief. On the contrary, the exercise of those powers is vindicated, not eroded, when confirmed by the Judicial Branch. Within the Constitution's separation-of-powers structure, few exercises of judicial power are as legitimate or as necessary as the responsibility to hear challenges to the authority of the Executive to imprison a person.

JUSTICE SOUTER, with whom Justices GINSBURG and BREYER join, concurring.

[A fact] insufficiently appreciated by the dissents is the length of the disputed imprisonments, some of the prisoners represented here today having been locked up for six years. Hence the hollow ring when the dissenters suggest that the Court is somehow precipitating the judiciary into reviewing claims that the military (subject to appeal to the Court of Appeals for the District of Columbia Circuit) could handle within some reasonable period of time. [After] six years of sustained executive detentions in Guantanamo, subject to habeas jurisdiction but without any actual habeas scrutiny, today's decision is no judicial victory, but an act of perseverance in trying to make habeas review, and the obligation of the courts to provide it, mean something of value both to prisoners and to the Nation.

CHIEF JUSTICE ROBERTS, with whom Justices SCALIA, THOMAS, and ALITO join, dissenting.

Today the Court strikes down as inadequate the most generous set of procedural protections ever afforded aliens detained by this country as enemy combatants. The political branches crafted these procedures amidst an ongoing military conflict, after much careful investigation and thorough debate. [I] believe the system the political branches constructed adequately protects any constitutional rights aliens captured abroad and detained as enemy combatants may enjoy. I therefore would dismiss these cases on that ground.

[CSRT] review is just the first tier of collateral review in the DTA system. The statute provides additional review in an Article III court. [A] *court* determines whether the CSRT procedures are constitutional, and a *court* determines whether those procedures were followed in a particular case. [The] Hamdi plurality concluded that this type of review would be enough to satisfy due process, even for citizens. Congress followed the Court's lead, only to find itself the victim of a constitutional bait and switch. [Hamdi] said the Constitution guarantees citizen detainees only "basic" procedural rights, and that the process for securing those rights can "be tailored to alleviate [the] uncommon potential to burden the Executive at a time of ongoing military conflict." [All told,] the DTA provides the prisoners held at Guantanamo Bay adequate opportunity to contest the bases of their detentions, which is all habeas corpus need allow.

[The] Court finds the DTA system an inadequate habeas substitute, for one central reason: Detainees are unable to introduce at the appeal stage exculpatory evidence discovered after the conclusion of their CSRT proceedings. [If] this is the most the Court can muster, the ice beneath its feet is thin indeed. [The] CSRT procedures provide ample opportunity for detainees to introduce exculpatory evidence—whether documentary in nature or from live witnesses—before the military tribunals. [The] Court's hand wringing over the DTA's treatment of later-discovered exculpatory evidence is the most it has to show after a roving search for constitutionally problematic scenarios. But "[t]he delicate power of pronouncing an Act of Congress unconstitutional," we have said, "is not to be exercised with reference to hypothetical cases thus imagined." The Court today invents a sort of reverse facial challenge and applies it with gusto: If there is *any* scenario in which the statute *might* be constitutionally infirm, the law must be struck down.

[The] majority rests its decision on abstract and hypothetical concerns. Step back and consider what, in the real world, Congress and the Executive have actually granted aliens captured by our Armed Forces overseas and found to be enemy combatants:

> The right to hear the bases of the charges against them, including a summary of any classified evidence.

> The ability to challenge the bases of their detention before military tribunals modeled after Geneva Convention procedures

> [The] right, before the CSRT, to testify, introduce evidence, call witnesses, question those the Government calls, and secure release, if and when appropriate.

> The right to the aid of a personal representative in arranging and presenting their cases before a CSRT.

> Before the D. C. Circuit, the right to employ counsel, challenge the factual record, contest the lower tribunal's legal determinations, ensure compliance with the Constitution and laws, and secure release, if any errors below establish their entitlement to such relief.

In sum, the DTA satisfies the majority's own criteria for assessing adequacy. This statutory scheme provides the combatants held at Guantanamo greater procedural protections than have ever been afforded alleged enemy detainees—whether citizens or aliens—in our national history.

Justice SCALIA, with whom THE CHIEF JUSTICE and Justices THOMAS and ALITO join, dissenting.

Today, for the first time in our Nation's history, the Court confers a constitutional right to habeas corpus on alien enemies detained abroad by our military forces in the course of an ongoing war. The Chief Justice's dissent, which I join, shows that the procedures prescribed by Congress in the Detainee Treatment Act provide the essential protections that habeas corpus guarantees; there has thus been no suspension of the writ, and no basis exists for judicial intervention beyond what the Act allows. My problem with today's opinion is more fundamental still: The writ of habeas corpus does not, and never has, run in favor of aliens abroad; the Suspension Clause thus has no application, and the Court's intervention in this military matter is entirely ultra vires.

[The] Suspension Clause of the Constitution provides: "The Privilege of the Writ of Habeas Corpus shall not be suspended, unless when in Cases of Rebellion or Invasion the public Safety may require it." Art. I, § 9, cl. 2. As a court of law operating under a written Constitution, our role is to determine whether there is a conflict between that Clause and the Military Commissions Act. A conflict arises only if the Suspension Clause preserves the privilege of the writ for aliens held by the United States military as enemy combatants at the base in Guantanamo Bay, located within the sovereign territory of Cuba.

[The] Court purports to derive from our precedents a "functional" test for the extraterritorial reach of the writ, which shows that the Military Commissions Act unconstitutionally restricts the scope of habeas. That is remarkable because the most pertinent of those precedents, Johnson v. Eisentrager, conclusively establishes the opposite. There we were confronted with the claims of 21 Germans held at Landsberg Prison, an American military facility located in the American Zone of occupation in postwar Germany. They had been captured in China, and an American military commission sitting there had convicted them of war crimes—collaborating with the Japanese after Germany's surrender. Like the petitioners here, the Germans claimed that their detentions violated the Constitution and international law, and sought a writ of habeas corpus. Writing for the Court, Justice Jackson held that American courts lacked habeas jurisdiction. Eisentrager thus held—*held* beyond any doubt—that the Constitution does not ensure habeas for aliens held by the United States in areas over which our Government is not sovereign. [Eisentrager] nowhere mentions a "functional" test, and the notion that it is based upon such a principle is patently false. [There] is simply no support for the Court's assertion that constitutional rights extend to aliens held outside U.S. sovereign territory, and Eisentrager could not be clearer that the privilege of habeas corpus does not extend to aliens abroad. By blatantly distorting Eisentrager, the Court avoids the difficulty of explaining why it should be overruled.

[Putting] aside the conclusive precedent of Eisentrager, it is clear that the original understanding of the Suspension Clause was that habeas corpus was not available to aliens abroad. It is entirely clear that, at English common law, the writ of habeas corpus did not extend beyond the sovereign territory of the Crown. To be sure, the writ had an "extraordinary territorial ambit," because it was a so-called "prerogative writ," which, unlike other writs, could extend beyond the realm of England to other places where the Crown was sovereign. But prerogative writs could not issue to foreign countries, even for British subjects; they were confined to the King's dominions—those areas over which the Crown was sovereign. [In sum,] *all* available historical evidence points to the conclusion that the writ would not have been available at common law for aliens captured and held outside the sovereign territory of the Crown.

[What] history teaches is confirmed by the nature of the limitations that the Constitution places upon suspension of the common-law writ. It can be suspended only "in Cases of Rebellion or Invasion." Art. I, § 9, cl. 2. The latter case (invasion) is plainly limited to the territory of the United States; and while it is conceivable that a rebellion could be mounted by American citizens abroad, surely the overwhelming majority of its occurrences would be domestic. [Because] I conclude that the text and history of the Suspension Clause provide no basis for our jurisdiction, I would affirm the Court of Appeals even if Eisentrager did not govern these cases.

CHAPTER 7

THE BILL OF RIGHTS AND THE POST–CIVIL WAR AMENDMENTS: "FUNDAMENTAL" RIGHTS AND THE "INCORPORATION" DISPUTE

SECTION 3.   THE "INCORPORATION" OF THE BILL OF RIGHTS THROUGH THE DUE PROCESS CLAUSE

Page 361.   Add after Note 3:

4. *The Right to Bear Arms.* The Second Amendment provides: "A well regulated Militia, being necessary to the security of a free State, the right of the people to keep and bear Arms, shall not be infringed." This is one of the original Bill of Rights never incorporated against the States through the Fourteenth Amendment Due Process Clause. In DISTRICT OF COLUMBIA v. HELLER, ___ U.S. ___, 128 S.Ct. 2783 (2008), the Supreme Court for the first time in our constitutional history enforced the Amendment as a matter of individual right unconnected with service in a militia. By a 5–4 majority, the Court invalidated a D.C. law that effectively banned the possession of handguns. Because D.C. is governed by the federal government, the Court did not need to reach the incorporation issue that will be posed by future challenges to state or city gun ordinances. Writing for the narrowly divided Court, Justice SCALIA, joined by Chief Justice Roberts and Justices Kennedy, Thomas and Alito, explained the late-breaking nature of the decision: "It should be unsurprising that such a significant matter has been for so long judicially unresolved. For most of our history, the Bill of Rights was not thought applicable to the States, and the Federal Government did not significantly regulate the possession of firearms by law-abiding citizens. Other provisions of the Bill of Rights have similarly remained unilluminated for lengthy periods."

Justice Scalia's majority opinion began by reviewing the linguistic and historical meaning of the right to keep and bear arms, concluding that it confers individual rather than collective rights and is unconnected to militia service: "The first salient feature of the operative clause is that it codifies a 'right of the people.' The unamended Constitution and the Bill of Rights use the phrase 'right of the people' two other times, in the First Amendment's Assembly-and-Petition Clause and in the Fourth Amendment's Search-and-Seizure Clause. The Ninth Amendment uses very similar terminology ('The enumeration in the Constitution, of certain rights, shall not be construed to deny or disparage others retained by the people'). All three of these instances unambiguously refer to individual rights, not 'collective' rights, or rights that may be exercised only through participation in some corporate body. [Reading] the Second Amendment as protecting only the right to 'keep and bear Arms' in an organized militia therefore fits poorly with the operative clause's description of the holder of that right as 'the people.' We start therefore with a strong presumption that the Second Amendment right is exercised individually and belongs to all Americans."

Turning to the meaning of the phrase "to keep and bear Arms," Justice Scalia concluded that "Arms" means the same now as in the 18th century: "The 1773 edition of Samuel Johnson's dictionary defined 'arms' as 'weapons of offence, or armour of defence.' [The] term was applied, then as now, to weapons that were not specifically designed for military use and were not employed in a military capacity." Again looking to Johnson's dictionary, he concluded further that "the most natural reading of 'keep Arms' in the Second Amendment is to 'have weapons,'" again with no necessary connection to a militia. And while he read the phrase "bear Arms" to imply the carrying of a weapon for the purpose of offensive or defensive confrontation, he suggested that this "in no way connotes participation in a structured military organization." Justice Scalia concluded: "Putting all of these textual elements together, we find that they guarantee the individual right to possess and carry weapons in case of confrontation. This meaning is strongly confirmed by the historical background of the Second Amendment. We look to this because it has always been widely understood that the Second Amendment, like the First and Fourth Amendments, codified a *pre-existing* right. The very text of the Second Amendment implicitly recognizes the pre-existence of the right and declares only that it 'shall not be infringed.'"

Turning to the prefatory clause, "A well regulated Militia, being necessary to the security of a free State," Justice Scalia asked "Does the preface fit with an operative clause that creates an individual right to keep and bear arms? It fits perfectly, once one knows the history that the founding generation knew. [That] history showed that the way tyrants had eliminated a militia consisting of all the able-bodied men was not by banning the militia but simply by taking away the people's arms, enabling a select militia or standing army to suppress political opponents. This is what had occurred in England that prompted codification of the right to have arms in the English Bill of Rights. [It] is therefore entirely sensible that the Second Amendment's prefatory clause announces the purpose for which the right was codified: to prevent elimination of the militia. The prefatory clause does not suggest that preserving the militia was the only reason Americans valued the ancient right; most undoubtedly thought it even more important for self-defense and hunting. But the threat that the new Federal Government would destroy the citizens' militia by taking away their arms was the reason that right—unlike some other English rights—was codified in a written Constitution."

Finding that post-Ratification history supported this historical account, Justice Scalia then turned to the aftermath of the Civil War, when "there was an outpouring of discussion of the Second Amendment in Congress and in public discourse, as people debated whether and how to secure constitutional rights for newly free slaves. [Blacks] were routinely disarmed by Southern States after the Civil War. Those who opposed these injustices frequently stated that they infringed blacks' constitutional right to keep and bear arms. Needless to say, the claim was not that blacks were being prohibited from carrying arms in an organized state militia. [It] was plainly the understanding in the post-Civil War Congress that the Second Amendment protected an individual right to use arms for self-defense.''

Justice Scalia's majority opinion cautioned that, ''[l]ike most rights, the right secured by the Second Amendment is not unlimited. From Blackstone through the 19th-century cases, commentators and courts routinely explained that the right was not a right to keep and carry any weapon whatsoever in any manner whatsoever and for whatever purpose.'' He noted the ''historical tradition of prohibiting the carrying of 'dangerous and unusual weapons.' '' But, turning to the D.C. law at issue, he found it incapable of constitutional defense: ''[T]he law totally bans handgun possession in the home. It also requires that any lawful firearm in the home be disassembled or bound by a trigger lock at all times, rendering it inoperable. [The] inherent right of self-defense has been central to the Second Amendment right. The handgun ban amounts to a prohibition of an entire class of 'arms' that is overwhelmingly chosen by American society for that lawful purpose. The prohibition extends, moreover, to the home, where the need for defense of self, family, and property is most acute. Under any of the standards of scrutiny that we have applied to enumerated constitutional rights, banning from the home 'the most preferred firearm in the nation to ''keep'' and use for protection of one's home and family,' would fail constitutional muster.'' He concluded: ''We are aware of the problem of handgun violence in this country. [The] Constitution leaves the District of Columbia a variety of tools for combating that problem, including some measures regulating handguns. But the enshrinement of constitutional rights necessarily takes certain policy choices off the table. These include the absolute prohibition of handguns held and used for self-defense in the home.''

Justice STEVENS wrote a dissent, joined by Justices Souter, Ginsburg and Breyer, taking a very different view of the founding text and history: ''The question presented by this case is not whether the Second Amendment protects a 'collective right' or an 'individual right.' Surely it protects a right that can be enforced by individuals. But a conclusion that the Second Amendment protects an individual right does not tell us anything about the scope of that right. Guns are used to hunt, for self-defense, to commit crimes, for sporting activities, and to perform military duties. The Second Amendment plainly does not protect the right to use a gun to rob a bank; it is equally clear that it *does* encompass the right to use weapons for certain military purposes. Whether it also protects the right to possess and use guns for nonmilitary purposes like hunting and personal self-defense is the question presented by this case. The text of the Amendment, its history, and our decision in United States v. Miller, 307 U.S. 174 (1939), provide a clear answer to that question.

''The Second Amendment was adopted to protect the right of the people of each of the several States to maintain a well-regulated militia. It was a response to concerns raised during the ratification of the Constitution that the power of Congress to disarm the state militias and create a national standing army posed an intolerable threat to the sovereignty of the several States. Neither the text of the Amendment nor the arguments advanced by its proponents evidenced the slightest interest in limiting any legislature's authority to regulate private civilian uses of firearms. Specifically, there is no indication that the Framers of the Amendment intended to enshrine the common-law right of self-defense in the Constitution. [The] view of the Amendment we took in Miller—that it protects the right to keep and bear arms for certain military purposes, but that it does not curtail the Legislature's power to regulate the nonmilitary use and ownership of weapons—is both the most natural reading of the Amendment's text and the interpretation most faithful to the history of its adoption."

Justice BREYER's separate dissent, joined by Justices Stevens, Souter and Ginsburg, agreed with Justice Stevens that the Amendment does not protect an interest in individual self-defense, but argued that, even assuming arguendo that it did, under an appropriate balancing of interests, D.C.'s regulation, "which focuses upon the presence of handguns in high-crime urban areas, represents a permissible legislative response to a serious, indeed life-threatening, problem."

CHAPTER 8

DUE PROCESS

SECTION 1. SUBSTANTIVE DUE PROCESS AND ECONOMIC LIBERTIES

Page 384.   Add to end of Note 3:

In EXXON SHIPPING CO. v. BAKER, ___ U.S. ___, 128 S.Ct. 2605 (2008), the Court imposed a limit on punitive damages as a matter of federal common law rather than substantive due process. The case involved a $2.5 billion jury verdict against Exxon for the catastrophic oil spill in 1993 by the ship Exxon Valdez, which caused extensive damage to the Alaska coastline and fishing grounds. Under federal maritime law, the Court held, punitive damages could be awarded only at most in a one-to-one ratio to compensatory damages. It accordingly capped punitive damages in the case at the equivalent of the $507.5 million compensatory damages award.

In his opinion for the Court, Justice SOUTER alluded to its substantive due process precedents: "Today's enquiry differs from due process review because the case arises under federal maritime jurisdiction, and we are reviewing a jury award for conformity with maritime law, rather than the outer limit allowed by due process; we are examining the verdict in the exercise of federal maritime common law authority, which precedes and should obviate any application of the constitutional standard. [Whatever] may be the constitutional significance of the unpredictability of high punitive awards, this feature of happenstance is in tension with the function of the awards as punitive, just because of the implication of unfairness that an eccentrically high punitive verdict carries in a system whose commonly held notion of law rests on a sense of fairness in dealing with one another. Thus, a penalty should be reasonably predictable in its severity, so that even Justice Holmes's 'bad man' can look ahead with some ability to know what the stakes are in choosing one course of action or another. And when the bad man's counterparts turn up from time to time, the penalty scheme they face ought to threaten them with a fair probability of suffering in like degree when they wreak like damage. The common sense of justice would surely bar penalties that reasonable people would think excessive for the harm caused in the circumstances."

Arriving at the 1:1 ratio after a detailed review of history, state law and empirical evidence, Justice Souter noted that "our explanation of the constitutional upper limit confirms that the 1:1 ratio is not too low. In State Farm, we said that a single-digit maximum is appropriate in all but the most exceptional of cases, and '[w]hen compensatory damages are substantial, then a lesser ratio, perhaps only equal to compensatory damages, can reach the outermost limit of the due process guarantee.'" Justices Stevens, Ginsburg and Breyer dissented from the decision to overturn the particular award at issue, reasoning either that Congress should set the rules in this area or that this was a special case warranting an exception from any rigid ratio.

CHAPTER 9

EQUAL PROTECTION

SECTION 4. THE "FUNDAMENTAL INTERESTS" BRANCH OF EQUAL PROTECTION

Page 643. Add after Note 2:

3. *Voter ID requirements.* What level of scrutiny should apply to a state law requiring voters to present specified forms of identification at the polls in order to vote? Are such requirements subject to facial challenge on the ground that they have the same de facto discriminatory effect as a poll tax? In CRAWFORD v. MARION COUNTY ELECTION BOARD, ___ U.S. ___, 128 S.Ct. 1610 (2008), the Supreme Court rejected a challenge to an Indiana law (SEA 483) requiring citizens voting in person to present government-issued photo identification. Justice STEVENS, writing for the Court in an opinion joined by Chief Justice Roberts and Justice Kennedy, declined to apply the strict scrutiny applied in Harper and instead engaged in a balancing of interests: "The State has identified several state interests that arguably justify the burdens that SEA 483 imposes on voters and potential voters. [Each] is unquestionably relevant to the State's interest in protecting the integrity and reliability of the electoral process. The first is the interest in deterring and detecting voter fraud. [The] only kind of voter fraud that SEA 483 addresses is in-person voter impersonation at polling places. The record contains no evidence of any such fraud actually occurring in Indiana at any time in its history. Moreover, petitioners argue that provisions of the Indiana Criminal Code punishing such conduct as a felony provide adequate protection against the risk that such conduct will occur in the future. It remains true, however, that flagrant examples of such fraud in other parts of the country have been documented throughout this Nation's history. [Not] only is the risk of voter fraud real but [it] could affect the outcome of a close election.

"[The] burdens that are relevant to the issue before us are those imposed on persons who are eligible to vote but do not possess a current photo identification that complies with the requirements of SEA 483. The fact that most voters already possess a valid driver's license, or some other form of acceptable identification, would not save the statute under our reasoning in Harper, if the State required voters to pay a tax or a fee to obtain a new photo identification. But [the] photo identification cards issued by Indiana's BMV [are] free. For most voters who need them, the inconvenience of making a trip to the BMV, gathering the required documents, and posing for a photograph surely does not qualify as a substantial burden on the right to vote, or even represent a significant increase over the usual burdens of voting. [The] severity of that burden is [mitigated] by the fact that, if eligible, voters without photo identification may cast provisional ballots that will ultimately be counted. To do so, however, they must travel to the circuit court clerk's office within 10 days to execute the required affidavit. It is unlikely that such a requirement would pose a constitutional problem unless it is wholly unjustified. And even assuming that the burden may not be justified as to a few voters, that conclusion is by no means sufficient to establish petitioners' right to [facial invalidation]."

Justice Stevens thus declined to rely on record evidence that SEA 483 had been particularly burdensome for some voters such as the disabled and the elderly. Nor did he take account of the fact that "all of the Republicans in the General Assembly voted in favor of SEA 483 and the Democrats were unanimous in opposing it," reasoning that, "if a nondiscriminatory law is supported by valid neutral justifications, those justifications should not be disregarded simply because partisan interests may have provided one motivation for the votes of individual legislators."

Justice SCALIA filed a concurrence in the judgment, joined by Justices Thomas and Alito, stressing that "the burden at issue is minimal and justified" and that strict scrutiny under Harper should not be employed, even in as-applied challenges, for "nonsevere, nondiscriminatory restrictions" on the right to vote—a possibility he believed the plurality had left open. He concluded that "the Indiana photo-identification law is a generally applicable, nondiscriminatory voting regulation, and our precedents refute the view that individual impacts are relevant to determining the severity of the burden it imposes. [The] Fourteenth Amendment does not regard neutral laws as invidious ones, even when their burdens purportedly fall disproportionately on a protected class. A fortiori it does not do so when, as here, the classes complaining of disparate impact are not even protected."

Justice SOUTER dissented, joined by Justice Ginsburg. Finding that "Indiana's 'Voter ID Law' threatens to impose nontrivial burdens on the voting right of tens of thousands of the State's citizens, and a significant percentage of those individuals are likely to be deterred from voting," he would have found the law unconstitutional even on a balancing analysis. Justice Souter explained: "Voting-rights cases raise two competing interests, the one side being the fundamental right to vote. The Judiciary is obliged to train a skeptical eye on any qualification of that right. See Reynolds. [The] travel costs and fees necessary to get one of the limited variety of federal or state photo identifications needed to cast a regular ballot under the Voter ID Law [will] affect voters according to their circumstances, with the average person probably viewing it as nothing more than an inconvenience. Poor, old, and disabled voters who do not drive a car, however, may find the trip prohibitive. [The] burden of traveling to a more distant BMV office rather than a conveniently located polling place is probably serious for many of the individuals who lack photo identification. They almost certainly will not own cars, and public transportation in Indiana is fairly limited.

"For those voters who can afford the roundtrip, a second financial hurdle appears: in order to get photo identification for the first time, they need to present 'a birth certificate, a certificate of naturalization, U.S. veterans photo identification, U.S. military photo identification, or a U.S. passport.' [Indiana] counties charge anywhere from $3 to $12 for a birth certificate, and that same price must usually be paid for a first-time passport, since a birth certificate is required to prove U.S. citizenship by birth. The total fees for a passport, moreover, are up to about $100. So most voters must pay at least one fee to get the ID necessary to cast a regular ballot. [Both] the travel costs and the fees are disproportionately heavy for, and thus disproportionately likely to deter, the poor, the old, and the immobile." The dissent found "that provisional ballots do not obviate the burdens of getting photo identification" because the "need to travel to the county seat each election amounts to a high hurdle." And finding that these burdens would deter or discourage a substantial number of Indiana voters, Justice Souter stated that Indiana's purported interests must withstand "a rigorous assessment."

Applying such review, Justice Souter's dissent found SEA 483 wanting, for even if preventing voter fraud is an important interest in the abstract, "the State has not come across a single instance of in-person voter impersonation fraud in all of Indiana's history." He concluded: "the Indiana statute crosses a line when it targets the poor and the weak. If the Court's decision in Harper v. Virginia Bd. of Elections stands for anything, it is that being poor has nothing to do with being qualified to vote. Harper made clear that '[t]o introduce wealth or payment of a fee as a measure of a voter's qualifications is to introduce a capricious or irrelevant factor.' The State's requirements here, that people without cars travel to a motor vehicle registry and that the poor who fail to do that get to their county seats within 10 days of every election, likewise translate into unjustified economic burdens uncomfortably close to the outright $1.50 fee we struck down 42 years ago. Like that fee, the onus of the Indiana law is illegitimate just because it correlates with no state interest so well as it does with the object of deterring poorer residents from exercising the franchise."

Justice BREYER filed a separate dissent, comparing the burden imposed by the Indiana statute to the poll tax struck down in Harper: "[A]n Indiana nondriver, most likely to be poor, elderly, or disabled, will find it difficult and expensive to travel to the Bureau of Motor Vehicles, particularly if he or she resides in one of the many Indiana counties lacking a public transportation system. [Many] of these individuals may be uncertain about how to obtain the underlying documentation, usually a passport or a birth certificate, upon which the statute insists. And some may find the costs associated with these documents unduly burdensome (up to $12 for a copy of a birth certificate; up to $100 for a passport). By way of comparison, this Court previously found unconstitutionally burdensome a poll tax of $1.50 (less than $10 today, inflation-adjusted). See Harper." He concluded that, "while the Constitution does not in general forbid Indiana from enacting a photo ID requirement, this statute imposes a disproportionate burden upon those without valid photo IDs."

CHAPTER 13

RIGHTS ANCILLARY TO FREEDOM OF SPEECH

SECTION 2. FREEDOM OF EXPRESSIVE ASSOCIATION

Page 1163.   Add to end of Note 2:

In NEW YORK STATE BOARD OF ELECTIONS v. LOPEZ TORRES, ___ U.S. ___, 128 S.Ct. 791 (2008), the Supreme Court rendered a unanimous judgment rejecting a challenge to a New York election law that required parties to select nominees to state trial court judgeships by a convention composed of delegates elected by party members. The challengers sought to compel primary elections for these seats. Justice SCALIA, writing for the Court, found nothing in the First Amendment that would entitle a challenger to so alter a party's selection process: "Respondents' real complaint is [that] the convention process that follows the delegate election does not give them a realistic chance to secure the party's nomination. The party leadership, they say, inevitably garners more votes for its slate of delegates (delegates uncommitted to any judicial nominee) than the unsupported candidate can amass for himself. And thus the leadership effectively determines the nominees. But this says nothing more than that the party leadership has more widespread support than a candidate not supported by the leadership. No New York law compels election of the leadership's slate— or, for that matter, compels the delegates elected on the leadership's slate to vote the way the leadership desires. And no state law prohibits an unsupported candidate from attending the convention and seeking to persuade the delegates to support her.

"Our cases invalidating ballot-access requirements have focused on the requirements themselves, and not on the manner in which political actors function under those requirements. See, e.g., Bullock v. Carter, Williams v. Rhodes, Anderson v. Celebrezze. Here respondents complain not of the state law, but of the voters' (and their elected delegates') preference for the choices of the party leadership." Justices Stevens and Kennedy each concurred separately, expressing doubts about the wisdom of the State's policy.

Page 1167.   Add to end of Note 4:

Eight years after deciding California Democratic Party v. Jones, the Supreme Court reached the opposite result in WASHINGTON STATE GRANGE v. WASHINGTON STATE REPUBLICAN PARTY, ___ U.S. ___, 128 S.Ct. 1184 (2008). This decision upheld against facial First Amendment challenge a Washington state law (I–872), enacted by voter initiative, providing that candidates must be identified on the primary ballot by their self-designated party preference, that voters may vote for any candidate, and that the two top vote-getters for each office advance to the general election regardless of a party's preference.

Writing for the 7–2 majority, Justice THOMAS, joined by Chief Justice Roberts and Justices Stevens, Souter, Ginsburg, Breyer, and Alito, explained why Jones was not controlling: "[U]nlike the California primary, the I–872 primary does not, by its terms, choose parties' nominees. The essence of nomination—the choice of a party representative—does not occur under I–872. The law never refers to the candidates as nominees of any party, nor does it treat them as such. To the contrary, the election regulations specifically provide that the primary 'does not serve to determine the nominees of a political party but serves to winnow the number of candidates to a final list of two for the general election.' The top two candidates from the primary election proceed to the general election regardless of their party preferences. Whether parties nominate their own candidates outside the state-run primary is simply irrelevant.

"At bottom, respondents' objection to I–872 is that voters will be confused by candidates' party-preference designations. [They] argue that even if voters do not assume that candidates on the general election ballot are the nominees of their parties, they will at least assume that the parties associate with, and approve of, them. This, they say, compels them to associate with candidates they do not endorse, alters the messages they wish to convey, and forces them to engage in counterspeech to disassociate themselves from the candidates and their positions on the issues. We reject each of these contentions for the same reason: They all depend, not on any facial requirement of I–872, but on the possibility that voters will be confused as to the meaning of the party-preference designation. But respondents' assertion that voters will misinterpret the party-preference designation is sheer speculation. [Of course,] it is *possible* that voters will misinterpret the candidates' party-preference designations as reflecting endorsement by the parties. But these cases involve a facial challenge, and we cannot strike down I–872 on its face based on the mere possibility of voter confusion." Finding no heavy burden on party or voter associational rights, the Court found no need for a compelling state interest, and found that, on appropriately deferential review, Washington's "asserted interest in providing voters with relevant information about the candidates on the ballot is easily sufficient to sustain I–872."

Justice SCALIA, joined by Justice Kennedy, dissented, finding Jones materially indistinguishable: "The Court makes much of the fact that the party names shown on the Washington ballot may be billed as mere statements of candidate 'preference.' To be sure, the party is not *itself* forced to display favor for someone it does not wish to associate with, as the Boy Scouts were arguably forced to do by employing the homosexual scoutmaster in Dale, and as the political parties were arguably forced to do by lending their ballot-endorsement as party nominee in Jones. But thrusting an unwelcome, self-proclaimed association upon the party on the election ballot itself is amply destructive of the party's associational rights. An individual's endorsement of a party shapes the voter's view of what the party stands for, no less than the party's endorsement of an individual shapes the voter's view of what the individual stands for. Not only is the party's message distorted, but its goodwill is hijacked. [There] is therefore 'no set of circumstances' under which Washington's law would not severely burden political parties.''

Justice Scalia's dissent would have found Washington's law incapable of withstanding the strict scrutiny he thus deemed appropriate: "Even if I were to assume, [that] Washington has a legitimate interest in telling voters on the ballot (above all other things) that a candidate *says* he favors a particular political party, and even if I were further to assume *(per impossibile)* that that interest was a compelling one, Washington would still have to 'narrowly tailor' its law to protect that interest with minimal intrusion upon the parties' associational rights. There has been no attempt to do that here. Washington could, for example, have permitted parties to disclaim on the general-election ballot the asserted association or to designate on the ballot their true nominees. The course the State has chosen makes sense only as an effort to use its monopoly power over the ballot to undermine the expressive activities of the political parties.''

SECTION 3.   MONEY AND POLITICAL CAMPAIGNS

Page 1205. Add after Note 3:

4. *Campaign finance challenges after WRTL: The "Millionaire's Amendment."* Did WRTL reveal a new 5–4 coalition on the Court more consistently inclined to invalidate campaign finance regulations challenged on free speech grounds? In DAVIS v. FEDERAL ELECTION COMM'N, ___ U.S. ___, 128 S.Ct. 2759 (2008), the Court invalidated § 319(a) of the Bipartisan Campaign Reform Act of 2002 (BCRA), the so-called "Millionaire's Amendment," which provided that, when a candidate's expenditure of personal funds exceeded $350,000, he would remain subject to normal contribution limits but his opponent would be permitted to receive individual contributions at treble the normal limit and unlimited coordinated party expenditures. The Court found the law barred by the First Amendment in an opinion by Justice ALITO, joined by Chief Justice Roberts and Justices Scalia, Kennedy and Thomas. Justice Alito wrote:

"If § 319(a) simply raised the contribution limits for all candidates, Davis' argument would plainly fail. [There is] no constitutional basis for attacking contribution limits on the ground that they are too high. [Section 319(a),] however, does not raise the contribution limits across the board. Rather, it raises the limits only for the non-self-financing candidate and does so only when the self-financing candidate's expenditure of personal funds causes the [$350,000] threshold to be exceeded. We have never upheld the constitutionality of a law that imposes different contribution limits for candidates who are competing against each other, and we agree with Davis that this scheme impermissibly burdens his First Amendment right to spend his own money for campaign speech.

"[Section 319(a)] requires a candidate to choose between the First Amendment right to engage in unfettered political speech and subjection to discriminatory fundraising limitations. Many candidates who can afford to make large personal expenditures to support their campaigns may choose to do so despite § 319(a), but they must shoulder a special and potentially significant burden if they make that choice. Under § 319(a), the vigorous exercise of the right to use personal funds to finance campaign speech produces fundraising advantages for opponents in the competitive context of electoral politics. [Because] § 319(a) imposes a substantial burden on the exercise of the First Amendment right to use personal funds for campaign speech, that provision cannot stand unless it is 'justified by a compelling state interest.' No such justification is present here.

"The burden imposed by § 319(a) on the expenditure of personal funds is not justified by any governmental interest in eliminating corruption or the perception of corruption. [Buckley] reasoned that reliance on personal funds *reduces* the threat of corruption, and therefore § 319(a), by discouraging use of personal funds, disserves the anticorruption interest. [The Government also] maintains that § 319(a)'s asymmetrical limits are justified because they 'level electoral opportunities for candidates of different personal wealth.' Our prior decisions, however, provide no support for the proposition that this is a legitimate government objective. [The] argument that a candidate's speech may be restricted in order to " 'level electoral opportunities' has ominous implications because it would permit Congress to arrogate the voters' authority to evaluate the strengths of candidates competing for office." The majority likewise invalidated the disclosure provisions of Section 319(a) as excessively burdening self-financed candidates' First Amendment rights.

A dissent by Justice STEVENS, joined by Justices, Souter, Ginsburg and Breyer, disagreed with the majority's First Amendment reasoning: "[T]he Millionaire's Amendment represents a modest, sensible, and plainly constitutional attempt by Congress to minimize the advantages enjoyed by wealthy candidates vis-a-vis those who must rely on the support of others to fund their pursuit of public office. [It] cannot be gainsaid that the twin rationales at the heart of the Millionaire's Amendment—reducing the importance of wealth as a criterion for public office and countering the perception that seats in the United States Congress are available for purchase by the wealthiest bidder—are important Government interests. It is also evident that Congress, in enacting the provision, crafted a solution that was carefully tailored to those concerns. [Enhancing] the speech of the millionaire's opponent, far from contravening the First Amendment, actually advances its core principles. If only one candidate can make himself heard, the voter's ability to make an informed choice is impaired."

Denying that preventing corruption is the sole government interest that can justify campaign contribution limits, Justice Stevens's dissent cited Austin for the proposition that "we have long recognized the strength of an independent governmental interest in reducing both the influence of wealth on the outcomes of elections, and the appearance that wealth alone dictates those results. [Although] the focus of our cases has been on aggregations of corporate rather than individual wealth, there is no reason that their logic—specifically, their concerns about the corrosive and distorting effects of wealth on our political process—is not equally applicable in the context of individual wealth." Thus, he concluded, "[m]inimizing the effect of concentrated wealth on our political process, and the concomitant interest in addressing the dangers that attend the perception that political power can be purchased, are [sufficiently] weighty objectives to justify" the Millionaire's Amendment.

In a portion of Justice Stevens's dissent in which he spoke only for himself, he expressed the view that Justice White's dissent in Buckley had proved correct, and that expenditure limits themselves should no longer be subject to strict scrutiny. To Justice Stevens, this conclusion provided independently sufficient grounds to uphold the Millionaire's Amendment: "If, as I have come to believe, Congress could attempt to reduce the millionaire candidate's advantage by imposing reasonable limits on *all* candidates' expenditures, it follows a fortiori that the eminently reasonable scheme before us today survives constitutional scrutiny."

†